MIRACLES

Proof of God's Power

MIRACLES
Proof of God's Power

by
T. L. Osborn

HARRISON HOUSE
P. O. Box 35035
Tulsa, OK 74135

Unless otherwise indicated, all Scripture quotations are taken from the *King James Version* of the Bible.

ISBN 0-89274-185-6
Copyright © 1981 by T. L. and/or Daisy Osborn
Printed in the United States of America
All Rights Reserved

MIRACLES
Proof of God's Power

"The love of the miraculous is not a mark of ignorance, but rather reveals man's intense desire to reach the unseen God."

— T. L. Osborn

The Author

Contents

1	The Fact of Miracles	9
2	Everybody Wants A Miracle	13
3	The Need for Miracles	17
4	Foundation for Miracles	19
5	Ministry of Miracles	23
6	Miracles As Evidence	27
7	Gospel of Miracles	31
8	Missions and Miracles	35
9	Jesus of Miracles	41
10	Miracles As Proof	45
11	Urgency of Miracles	49
12	The Miracle Witness	53
13	Miracles for Multitudes	57
14	Questions about Miracles	61
15	Miracles to Shake the World	65
16	Miracles Around the World	71
17	Miracles for Everybody	75
18	Miracles for You	77

1
The Fact of Miracles

Ministers and laymen, both at home and abroad, often ask us to share with them the secrets which we consider most vital to reach the unevangelized millions of our generation. The answer to their question is found in the life and ministry of Christ and of the Early Church.

When Jesus began His public ministry, it was **a ministry of miracles.**

His conception, birth, life, wisdom and teachings, ministry, death, resurrection, appearances, and ascension — **all were astounding and undeniable miracles.**

When the Church began her ministry, it was **a ministry of miracles.**

A stream of miracles flowed from the hands of the Apostles, upsetting religious systems of that day to the extent that even the Christ-rejecting Roman government trembled.

The Church had made a discovery: Christ, Whom God had raised from the dead, had the same power and worked the same miracles in response to their command, when given in His Name, as He did before He was condemned and killed. He was alive again! He lived in them! He had not changed!

By Jesus' Name, the sick were healed, the dead were raised, and demons were cast out!

Those first years of Early Church history, as recorded in the *Acts of the Apostles,* were example years for the *Acts of the Church* until the return of her Lord and Master. This was primitive Christianity!

If we do not have the supernatural in Christianity, we have nothing to offer the unbeliever except a religion. **True Christianity is not a religion**.

Religion is only a form, a ceremonial observance — **Christianity is life**.

Christianity is the **heart** and **nature of Jesus Christ** being manifested in a person.

Christianity is a **miracle-life**. It *began* in miracles; it is *based* on a succession of miracles; it is *propagated* by miracles. It is the only life which will satisfy the hunger of men and women everywhere.

The Bible is a miracle book — a record of divine happenings. Beginning with Abraham, all of the major characters of Old Testament history were *miracle-workers*; or rather, God wrought miracles in response to their daring and active faith.

The purpose of these miracles was to separate the people from dead gods and convert them to worship the Living God.

When miracles ended, the people lapsed into the worship of other gods and returned to the true and living God only after another series of astounding miracles.

Human beings have not changed. I know because for over three decades, in nearly seventy nations, we have carried the Gospel to millions, face-to-face. Multitudes of from 20,000 to over 200,000 have thronged our meetings and have turned to the Lord because of the miracles they have witnessed.

2
Everybody Wants A Miracle

Humanity wants a living God. Men and women crave a miracle.

Wherever there arises a man or woman whose prayers are heard and answered, greater crowds will flock to hear them than to hear the most famous philosopher or statesman in the world.

This love of the miraculous is not a mark of ignorance, but rather reveals man's intense desire to reach the unseen God. **Man wants to see God in action.**

From the beginning, in fact, God's purpose and plan for man was that he have supernatural ability. He was created with the aspirations, desires, and demands for supernatural authority. In Genesis 1:28, God said to man and to woman, *Subdue . . . and have dominion.*

Some tell us that education will take the place of miracles, that the Church no longer needs the supernatural power of God. However, education does not eliminate the desire for the miraculous in man.

How little they realize that such teaching simply becomes the laughingstock of the Enemy.

One mighty miracle today, in the Name of Jesus Christ, is worth more than a lifetime of theoretical pedagogy.

Nations have never been rescued from their sins and reproaches by philosophical oratory, by medical missions or ecclesiastical indoctrination; but by humble men and women who have had a new vision of the Christ Who is the *same yesterday, and to day, and for ever* (Heb. 13:8).

Every real spiritual awakening that has honored Christ and His Word has been attested by dynamic miracles. It is impossible to properly honor God's Word and not see miracles.

All normal people crave the supernatural. They long to see the manifestation of the power of God.

Even an atheistic professor, who denies any existence of God, will edge into the crowd to watch a miracle. A dead orthodoxy has no resurrection power within it, no miracle-working force back of it.

People are willing to put up with extravagances and some fanaticism in order to get a little touch of the supernatural God.

Cultured men and women will listen to an uneducated preacher because he (or she) has faith in the Living God. He prays, and he gets the answer!

People tell us that we do not need miracles today, that education will take their place; but they are fooled by the Adversary, deluded by Satan. They reveal their lack of understanding of the nature and heart-hunger of men and women.

This heart-hunger for the miraculous is deep-seated in humanity, regardless of nationality or background, because a human being is the offspring of the miracle God.

People want miracles today as much as they ever did. When they see God's Word confirmed by miracles, they know it is true and they turn to the Lord.

3
The Need for Miracles

Jesus Christ is as much a miracle-worker now as He ever was; and humanity needs His miracle touch now more than ever.

There must be a return to the Christ-life. He must be allowed to live in us, in His power and in His personal presence. That alone is true Christianity. All else in religion is an impersonal ceremony, offering nothing but a ritual and a lifeless formality to its adherents.

Our slogan must be: *Back to the Living, Miracle-working Christ.*

Wherever a man or a woman acts on God's Word in bold faith, the place will be crowded by throngs of people, eager to see

Christ's miracle-performing power in evidence.

Jesus attracted the multitudes by miracles; and wherever miracles are wrought in His Name today, He does the same. He is the same yesterday, today, and forever!

If we return to Bible preaching, we will get Bible results.

If we preach as the Early Church preached, we will get the same results, regardless of the area or the country in which we minister.

Unnumbered tens of thousands of Buddhists, Shintoists, Hindus, Moslems, fetish worshippers, and followers of other religions have believed on Jesus Christ and turned to Him in our crusades around the world, because they saw the proof of His living presence through the miracles which He wrought.

4
Foundation for Miracles

The Bible says, *Faith cometh by hearing . . . the word of God* (Rom. 10:17).

Today, faith *leaveth* by hearing the word of the theologian, and unbelief *cometh* by hearing the traditionalist.

You may proclaim a week of fasting, but this will not bring the miraculous into evidence if you teach the wrong message.

You may call whole nights of prayer, but it will be of no avail if your preaching is wrong.

Spiritual awakening must begin in the preacher, in the missionary, in the leader. The message must be right, or all else is vain.

The preacher, at home or abroad, must be willing to adjust his thinking, his preaching, and his actions. Otherwise, spiritual renewal under his or her ministry will never come.

Faith cometh by hearing . . . the word of God — not by teaching the traditions of men.

Jesus told the Pharisees that they were *making the word of God of none effect* through their traditions. (Mark 7:13.)

Unless the preacher, the missionary, or the leader is willing to surrender ideas, or methods, or teaching, or traditions which are not based on *thus saith the Word*, spiritual awakening cannot develop under his or her ministry. If a member does receive new light from God, the preaching will suppress it.

We cannot teach the ideas of modern theology and get Bible results. We cannot use the methods of an unscriptural missionary policy and win the non-Christian to Christ.

If you want to reap the fruit of faith, you must sow the seed of faith, which is the Word of God. (Luke 8:11.)

The sick will be healed, sinners will be converted, and unbelievers will turn to Christ in **any** locality, when the Gospel in its simplicity is proclaimed. Then when actions correspond with that message, it opens the way for Christ in His power to confirm His Word.

When you proclaim the truth, you cannot shut out the miraculous.

Jesus said, *Ye shall know the truth, and the truth shall make you free* (John 8:32).

God sent His Word and it healed them. (Ps. 107:20.) Young's translation says, *He sendeth his word and healeth them.*

God's promises are *life unto those that find them, and health to all their flesh* (Prov. 4:22).

God's Word is His voice speaking to you individually. Read His promises in the Bible. Accept them personally—as though the Lord were having a private conversation with you.

Do whatever He tells you to do and expect Him to do what He says He will do. **That is the foundation for real living faith**.

Believe His promises. Think about them. Hear them in your mind. Speak them with your lips. Act upon them in simple child-like faith and God will fulfill them in your life by a miracle today—now.

5
Ministry of Miracles

Amongst the thousands at home and abroad who have been miraculously healed by our Lord under this ministry, only a small percentage of them have been individually prayed for. Most have been healed through their own faith which was automatically produced in their own hearts while meditating on the Bible truths we presented from the platform or from the printed page.

In nearly seventy countries during more than three decades of world ministry, I have discovered that almost any member of any church knows about Paul's thorn, Job's boils, Timothy's sore stomach, the teaching of sickness as God's chastisement, and the idea of suffering sickness for the glory of God.

But very few of them can quote a Scripture in the Bible that definitely promises them healing. This is because preachers, missionaries, and teachers are not proclaiming these vital promises.

They are not teaching God's covenant of healing, His promises that reveal the believer's position of authority over Satan and Satan-made disease, the Christian's throne rights in prayer, Satan's legal and total defeat at Calvary, the believer's true ministry, Christ's bearing of our diseases and pains, or our legal right to health and abundant living.

Instead, they are teaching excuses for not being healed and reasons for remaining sick.

There are many truths of healing clearly and positively taught in the Bible. Without these truths, one has nothing upon which to base his or her faith.

If preachers or missionaries or teachers do not teach these truths, the people cannot know them.

If the people do not know them, there can be no faith for miracles.

If there is no faith, miracles will not be wrought.

If miracles are not wrought, there is nothing to draw unbelievers or non-Christians to hear the Gospel, nor to persuade them to believe it.

We must recognize the indisputable value of miracles! They are a witness of God's power, evidence of the truth of the Gospel which Jesus preached.

Without miracles, Christianity is no more than another religion. Real Christianity is *not a religion; it is a LIFE!* It is the *only* form of worship in which the object worshipped dwells in the heart of the worshipper.

No Hindu, Shintoist, or Buddhist ever claimed that the diety he worshipped dwelled inside of him. That would be sacrilegious.

Yet, *that* is precisely the very foundation of *Christianity* — Jesus dwelling in our hearts by faith. *Christ IN YOU, the hope of glory* (Col. 1:27).

Miracles wrought in the Name of Jesus Christ are the only real evidence **people can see that Christ is risen from the dead according to the Scriptures.** If He is risen, He will do the things He did before He was killed. **Miracles are the proof**.

6
Miracles As Evidence

And this gospel of the kingdom shall be preached in all the world for a witness unto all nations and then shall the end come (Matt. 24:14).

These words were spoken by Jesus Christ to His disciples in answer to their questions: *Tell us, when shall these things be? and what shall be the sign of thy coming, and of the end of the world?* (v. 3.)

He told them to beware of deceivers and of those who claim to be Christ. He said that they would hear of wars, earthquakes, and pestilence; that some of them would be hated and even killed for His

Name's sake; that there would be false prophets and that the love of many would wax cold because of abounding iniquity.

Then, after all of these signs, He gave them **the main sign of His coming:** *This gospel of the kingdom shall be preached in all the world for a witness unto all nations; and then shall the end come.*

When over half of the inhabitants of the world have not yet heard the Name of Jesus, much less *this Gospel of the Kingdom*, we cannot say that this sign has been fulfilled.

In Mark 13:10, Jesus said, *The gospel must first be published among all nations.*

When over half of the tribes of the world have not yet had a single portion of the Gospel translated into their languages, we cannot say that this has come to pass.

Behold, the bridegroom cometh (Matt. 25:6), and over half of our generation has not yet heard His Name mentioned!

There is much to be done and it must be done quickly!

The storm clouds of the evening are swiftly gathering, and the ripened grain of millions of souls will be swept into darkness unless we respond quickly. We **must** share the Good News with them! They **must** have an opportunity! The Gospel **must** first be published among all nations!

Why should **anyone** hear the Gospel **twice** before **everyone** has heard it **once?**

The supreme task of the Church is the evangelization of the world!

That was Christ's final order, His Great Commission, the purpose for which He sent forth His disciples!

My wife and I have already given over three decades to proclaim this mighty Gospel to nearly seventy nations.

For years, we have published *a ton* of Gospel literature *per day,* in 132 languages.

We have sponsored over 20,000 national preachers as full-time missionaries to their own unreached tribes and villages; they have established over one new self-supporting church *per day.*

We have provided millions of books, tens of thousands of crusade sermon tapes and documentary miracle films around the world—plus our own campaigns. Why? We *must* reach the world with *this* Gospel.

7
Gospel of Miracles

What is *this Gospel of the Kingdom?*

It is the same Gospel that Jesus Christ preached, the same as His disciples preached.

When Jesus told His disciples to go forth, He said, *As ye go, preach, saying, The kingdom of heaven is at hand.*

With that message, He told them to *heal the sick, cleanse the lepers, raise the dead, cast out devils: freely ye have received, freely give* (Matt. 10:7,8). These signs were evidence of this Gospel of the Kingdom.

And Jesus went about all the cities and villages teaching in their synagogues, and preaching the gospel of the kingdom, and healing every sickness and every disease among the people (Matt. 9:35).

When Jesus preached the Gospel of the Kingdom, He *always* healed the sick!

And he was casting out a devil . . . and it came to pass, when the devil was gone out . . . the people wondered (Luke 11:14). And Jesus said, *If I cast out devils by the Spirit of God, then the kingdom of God is come unto you* (Matt. 12:28).

Jesus proved that when the Gospel of the Kingdom is preached, devils are cast out and the sick are healed.

It is this Gospel of the Kingdom — preached in the power of the Spirit of God, confirmed by signs and wonders and divers miracles — that is bringing to pass **the greatest**

worldwide awareness of the power and living presence of Jesus Christ in history.

In the past, there have been certain countries which have received mighty visitations of the Lord's power. Now and then, here and there, a servant of God has arisen; but in these last days, nation after nation is being literally swept by the miraculous demonstration of **Jesus Christ in action.**

Not only is *one* servant of God being used, literally *scores* of both men and women are now preaching to multitudes — not just in *one* country, but in *almost every nation* under the sun which has religious liberty.

God is confirming the Word preached with signs and wonders, and a return to faith in God is the result!

In a recent crusade, a leper was cleansed by a miracle of God. Her hands and feet had degenerated and dropped off, leaving only stubs. Also, she was paralyzed. She crawled on her knees and stubbed hands and begged at the big market gateway.

She was instantly cured the first night she attended our crusade. The next day, thousands jammed the streets and the city was in an uproar as Miriam Gare walked and ran (on her stubbed legs), with her flesh clean and pure again, glorifying God publicly.

We assisted in having her fitted with special shoes and the District Commissioner wrote to tell us that this notable miracle had caused the entire district to know that Christ is alive today. **This is the Gospel with evidence.**

8
Missions and Miracles

In 1945, my wife and I, with our baby boy, sailed to India with a burning desire to preach Christ to those of other lands.

Though we had no previous experience abroad, we know now that the Holy Spirit was guiding us. Our plan was to immediately engage a national interpreter, build a large but simple palm-leaf shelter, conduct big crusades, and establish new churches. If we had done that, success would have been inevitable.

But instead, we listened to traditional missionaries. They discredited our plans and insisted that the most important thing for us to do was to study the language. They said we should not expect to accomplish much for the first three years.

Our better judgment reacted to this negativism; but having had no experience of our own abroad, we tried to convince ourselves that they knew best.

Throughout the winter we sat, doing nothing, but studying an occasional lesson in Hindustani. Once a week I went to the little mission and printed on a blackboard the title of the sermon the missionary proposed to deliver.

There was no vision. The mission was open only once a week — at 6:00 p.m. on Sunday for an hour-and-a-half. The meeting was never attended by more than ten or fifteen persons.

We sold some of our belongings for enough money to go to another city where we encountered a similar condition. The doors of the church there were opened at six o'clock on Sunday evening when, for a short time, a little group of Christians gathered to go through their usual routine.

I was engaged to conduct a "series of meetings," but was advised against making an invitation for sinners to come forward. As the missionary explained: "We just do things differently here than we do in the States."

Finally, on the last night of those meetings, I decided that, regardless of their methods, I would give the listeners an opportunity to accept Christ.

At the close of my message, I called for those who wanted to be saved to come forward, to kneel, and to receive the Lord. Eleven Indians immediately responded!

They fell on their knees, weeping, and received Jesus Christ.

Upon reaching the missionary's home after the service, we found him and his wife rejoicing. His wife was saying, "Honey, the meeting tonight has proven that if we preach and act like we do in the States, the same results will follow here."

As I recall those experiences in India, I have one major regret. Though I was only 21 years old and had no experience, I regret that I allowed anyone to detour me from the method which God had impressed upon me. The direction He had originally given me would have inevitably brought success.

We finally returned to the United States because we realized that, under those circumstances, we could never convince the non-

Christians that Jesus Christ was alive. We needed miracles to prove His power. So we fasted and prayed many days.

We had seen the masses.

We knew that, if they were ever to be reached with the Gospel in a really effective way, a new breed of missionary must arise.

We believed in miracles but did not know how to bring them about in our ministry. It was clear to us that if the blind could be made to see, the deaf to hear, the lame to walk, and the lepers to be cleansed, we knew that multiplied thousands would believe on the Lord and be saved.

But no one seemed to think that way. No one encouraged us. Everyone seemed to be content to relegate miracles to Bible times, while the masses of humanity lived and died without ever hearing a Gospel message confirmed by signs, miracles, and wonders.

We felt alone, helpless, and defeated; but, thank God, we did not surrender. We knew that the real *Mission* of Jesus Christ in the world was a *Mission* of *Miracles*, so we prayed and fasted—and God heard our prayers.

9
Jesus of Miracles

One morning, Jesus appeared to me. I knew He was alive and had all power.

Shortly after that experience, a man with a powerful miracle ministry came to Portland, Oregon, where we had settled down to pastor a church. Seeing his marvelous ministry, we knew that God would do the same miracles through any man or woman who would proclaim His simple promises and dare to act upon His written Word of power.

We determined to be at least two more vessels through which God could manifest His power.

As God began to show forth His mighty works in our ministry here in America, the unevangelized masses of other lands began anew to pass before our minds. With Christ's power in evidence — casting out devils and healing the sick — we knew the non-Christians could be won to Him by the masses.

Since then, we have ministered abroad as God has directed us, in nearly seventy nations. Unsuccessful missionary procedures have not been observed, nor have the negative ideas of people been allowed to hinder us. Instead, we have done what God had impressed us to do in India: We have engaged interpreters, rolled up our sleeves, and gone to work proclaiming Christ as the Savior and Healer of *all* who will call upon and serve Him.

Indeed, the results have been staggering and overwhelming: Hundreds of thousands of souls have accepted Christ, because they **heard** and **saw the miracles wrought in Jesus' Name.**

Jesus said, *This gospel of the kingdom shall be preached in all the world, as a witness, then shall the end come.*

Our ministry was revolutionized from the day we learned that Jesus Christ wanted to *work with us*, just like He had worked with His followers (after His resurrection), *confirming the word with signs following* (Mark 16:20).

In nearly seventy nations, we have not seen an exception—from cultured Europe to primitive New Guinea, from America to Africa, from Tanzania to Indonesia.

We have constructed our platforms on large fields or parks or in stadiums—outside where the peoples of all religions can assemble freely. We have kept our message simple: *Jesus Christ is the same yesterday, and to day, and for ever* (Heb. 13:8).

We have told the masses the things that happened to people who came to Jesus Christ in Bible days. We have said: *Come to Him like they came, believe on Him like they believed, call on Him like they called, cry like they cried, repent like they repented, pray like they prayed, act like they acted, AND YOU WILL RECEIVE WHAT THEY RECEIVED.*

Countless tens of thousands have been saved and healed as a result, because the *Jesus of Miracles* has never changed.

10
Miracles As Proof

I noticed one day that this word *witness* in the original means "something evidential; with proof or with evidence." This Gospel of the Kingdom shall be proclaimed to all the world **with evidence**.

This discovery increased the burning conviction of my heart — that our ministry today *must* be a replica of the ministry of Jesus Christ, that anything less is not *this Gospel with evidence.*

When John's disciples inquired as to whether or not Jesus was the Christ, they were instructed to *go and shew John again those things which ye do hear and see: the blind receive their sight, and the lame walk, the lepers are cleansed, and the deaf hear, the dead are raised up, and the poor have the gospel preached to them* (Matt. 11:4,5).

Did you notice it? Jesus said, "Tell John what you *hear* and *see!*"

They *heard* the Gospel preached.

They *saw* the blind receive their sight.

They *saw* the lame walk.

They *saw* the miracles!

Jesus' message was with evidence. His Gospel was with proof! His preaching was with demonstration!

There could be no doubt that He was the Christ!

Christian messengers have gone throughout the world, but not enough of them have *demonstrated* what they preach or teach. Consequently, many of them have preached their sermons year after year, seeing very few souls converted.

On the other hand, where men and women have boldly proclaimed Christ in all of His power today, unbelievers have been converted by the thousands.

The Gospel of the Kingdom *must be proclaimed with evidence. It must be preached as a witness. It is always the witness with the proof who convinces the court.*

When Philip went down to the unbelieving city of Samaria, he *preached Christ unto them. And the people with one accord gave heed unto those things which Philip spake, hearing and seeing the miracles which he did. For unclean spirits . . . came out of many that were possessed with them: and many taken with palsies, and that were lame, were healed. And there was great joy in that city* (Acts 8:5-8).

Notice: He *preached Christ* and he did it *with evidence!*

His message was *as a witness!*

Miracles *testified* to his sermons!

The witness convinced the city!

They all gave heed, *hearing* the message and *seeing* the miracles. A very large city was affected. It was not enough to hear the message, nor is that enough today; they had to *see* the miracles which bore *evidence* that Philip was preaching the truth. And today, it is the miracles which *witness* to the Gospel.

11
Urgency of Miracles

Always remember: **The evidence is essential.**

More can be accomplished in one year of *preaching and teaching the Gospel with evidence* than in a hundred years of ministry without the proof!

Paul testified that Christ wrought *mighty signs and wonders* through him by the power of the Spirit of God, which *made the Gentiles obedient* by *word* and *deed.* (Rom. 15:18,19.)

Hebrews 2:3,4 tells of our *great salvation* which was first *spoken* by the Lord, and was *confirmed* unto us by them that heard him — God also *bearing them witness,* both with *signs* and *wonders,* and with *divers miracles,* and *gifts of the Holy Ghost.*

Again, the Gospel was *with evidence!* Their message was *with proof!*

What the world needs are Christians who, like Paul, preach *not with enticing words of man's wisdom, but in demonstration of the Spirit and of power: that your faith should not stand in the wisdom of men, but in the power of God* (1 Cor. 2:4,5).

The world **must** hear this Gospel as a **witness!**

The Good News **must** be proclaimed with **proof** — with **evidence!**

Fancy sermons and elaborate discourses have no place. They draw no audience in this day of world evangelism. There is no place for such in the ministry of the Holy Ghost.

People's hearts are crying for rugged men and women of daring faith who will proclaim the power of the Holy Ghost — messengers whose preaching is coupled with mighty demonstration of signs and miracles as *evidence*, as a *witness*, of the Living Christ.

Only this Gospel of the Kingdom, preached as a witness, can be the means of evangelizing the world.

A Catholic priest attended one of our South American crusades. It was the first time for him to see the message of the Gospel confirmed by miracles. He was captivated by the simplicity of it all. In deep repentance for his past sins and unbelief, he fell on his face, among the people on the field, and was gloriously *born again*.

He testified before the multitude of 75,000 people in a weeping and trembling voice. He said: *When I came to this field, I saw no golden altar and candlesticks. I saw no professional clergyman. All I saw was an open, crude, wooden platform, a Bible, and a preacher of faith. And I saw Jesus Christ working with that preacher, confirming His Gospel with power and miracles.*

A missionary of a historical church organization said after our crusade in his city: *More souls have been saved in these three weeks than in thirty years of missions without miracles.*

12
The Miracle Witness

I shall never forget when I discovered that the word *witness* is the same word used in describing the "tabernacles of witness" for God's people in the wilderness.

This tent was called the "tabernacle of witness" because for twenty-four hours of every day **God's miraculous power was in evidence there**. In the Holiest Place, there existed perpetually the **miraculous presence of Jehovah-God**.

Other nations could build tents like the people of Israel did. They could collect the same materials and use the same metals; but one thing would be missing: **the**

shekinah glory of God's presence, the miraculous witness of Jehovah.

Continually, God was present! His glory was in evidence! It was the "tabernacle of witness"!

Jesus said, *Ye shall receive power, after that the Holy Ghost is come upon you: and ye shall be witnesses unto me* (Acts 1:8).

Paul wrote, *Know ye not that your body is the temple of the Holy Ghost?* (1 Cor. 6:19).

Now we are *His witnesses!* We are *tabernacles of witness!* **God's miraculous power must be perpetually in evidence in our lives!** We must bear Holy Ghost testimony!

Having been arrested for bringing healing to a cripple through the power of the Holy Ghost, Peter stood before a court of pious religious dignitaries and declared: "We are His *witnesses!*"

Those were the words used by Peter to describe the ministry of a true messenger of the Gospel: *We are His witnesses!*

Others may preach; they may deliver their discourses; but they lack the *power to witness.*

Without Holy Ghost power, there will be no miracle evidence!

The Holy Shekinah of God's miraculous presence *must* be in our lives if we are to see the results.

It is one thing to say, "I am a minister." It is another thing to say, "I am *His witness.*"

The greatest honor, the greatest calling on earth, is to be a *witness* for Jesus Christ.

Christianity has always been proclaimed and promulgated by *witnesses, confessors, testifiers* — by those who have met Jesus Christ and have experienced His love and power in their lives.

The early Christians were *commanded not to speak at all nor teach in the name of Jesus* (Acts 4:18).

But they *answered and said. . . Whether it be right in the sight of God to hearken unto you more than unto God, judge ye. For we cannot but speak the things which we have seen and heard* (Acts 4:19,20).

That is the Miracle Witness we must give to our world. That is why the power of the Holy Ghost is in us. We are "tabernacles of witness" through whom God's power and glory is manifested to give proof that Jesus Christ is alive, real, and present in the now.

13
Miracles for Multitudes

Mark 16:20 says, *They went forth, and preached every where, the Lord working with them, and confirming the word with signs following.*

Those were messengers *with evidence!* Their sermons were *demonstrated!* The Gospel preached by them was as *a witness!* They were preachers with power — full of God, full of faith, full of the Holy Ghost! They were *witnesses* for Christ!

Miracles were commonplace in those days!

Modern theologians tell us that we can believe on the Lord and be saved; yet at the same time, they are against the supernatural and deny miracles today. How unfortunate for them and for their listeners that they have not yet tasted the miraculous ministry of Christ for the Church today!

When those New Testament preachers arrived in town, the people said, *These that have turned the world upside down have come hither also* (Acts 17:6), and their words were not meant as a compliment.

How those unbelieving religious leaders of that day were frustrated upon hearing that Paul or Peter had arrived in their city!

When we arrived in a certain nation, some Protestant missionaries from the United States, unaware of God's miracle ministry abroad today, began a secret campaign to influence national pastors, declaring: "This man Osborn will cause division and confusion; it were better if he had never come to this city."

They worked diligently, going from house to house, trying to prevent this great campaign. Some were influenced by their counsel; but most of the local churches enthusiastically participated in the enormous crusade, and their churches overflowed with hundreds of new converts.

As evidence of the Gospel, many miracles, signs, and wonders were wrought, causing thousands to accept Christ as their Savior.

The Bible is our best example of **God's power in demonstration.** Wherever the preachers of the Early Church declared the Gospel, Christ confirmed their message with the miraculous.

Whether it was Peter in traditional Jerusalem, Philip in immoral Samaria, or Paul on the pagan island of Melita, the same results always followed: They proclaimed the Gospel; miracles were in evidence; multitudes believed and were added to the Church.

Acts 6:8,15 says, *Stephen, full of faith and power, did great wonders and miracles among the people . . . and all that sat in the council, looking stedfastly on him, saw his face as it had been the face of an angel.*

Stephen was *a witness!*
His sermons were *demonstrated!*
His preaching was *with power!*

14
Questions about Miracles

What kind of Bible would we have without an Elijah raising the dead and calling down fire from heaven?

What kind of Bible would we have without a Daniel praying in the lions' den and being unharmed — or without the three Hebrew children having faith to be delivered from a fiery furnace?

What kind of Gospel would we have without a compassionate Christ healing the sick, cleansing the lepers, raising the dead, and giving sight to the blind?

What kind of Early Church would we have without Peter raising the cripple, then gathering the sick on beds and on couches in the main streets of Jerusalem to be healed?

What kind of example would Paul be without healing the sick, commanding the impotent man to arise, and casting out the devils from the fortune-telling woman?

What kind of commission would we have without Christ's orders to cast out devils in His Name and to lay hands on the sick for their recovery? Or without His promise that serpents shall not harm you, nor shall any poisonous drink do you hurt?

Take these promises and miracles out of the Bible and what is left?

What kind of preacher do you have today who is opposed to the supernatural in his ministry?

What kind of preaching do you have without miracles in evidence?

What kind of missionary must people of other nations listen to who is against the miraculous today?

Without the evidence of God's power in the Bible, nothing is left but a ritualistic form of religious worship which can give no life, solve no problems, heal no sicknesses, and produce no new births among its adherents.

Jesus spoke in tough terms as He said: *Woe unto you, scribes and Pharisees, hypocrites! for ye compass sea and land to make one proselyte, and when he is made, ye make him twofold more the child of hell than yourselves* (Matt. 23:15).

I urge Christian men and women to an unyielding resolve that the Gospel with *evidence* shall be our message. We shall go forth and proclaim the Gospel — *this Gospel of the Kingdom!* We shall be witnesses with *proof* and we shall reap a harvest of lost souls for Christ as our reward.

And we have done it!

From one extremity of this globe to the other, the signs and miracles which have confirmed the Gospel we have proclaimed have caused unnumbered multitudes to believe on Jesus Christ and to receive Him as Savior and as Lord of their lives.

That is our mission: *to open their eyes, and to turn them from darkness to light, and from the power of Satan unto God, that they may receive forgiveness of sins* (Acts 26:18).

15
Miracles to Shake the World

When they had prayed, the place was shaken where they were assembled together . . . and with great power (of the Holy Ghost) gave the apostles witness of the resurrection of the Lord Jesus: and great grace was upon them all (Acts 4:31,33).

These were preachers with power — *witnesses with evidence!*

And by the hands of the apostles were many signs and wonders wrought among the people . . . and believers were the more added to the Lord, multitudes both of men and women (Acts 5:12,14).

Why were these multitudes added to the Lord? Because of the

signs and wonders that were done in His Name.

The Early Church operated on one principle: *We ought to obey God rather than men* (Acts 5:29), *for we cannot but speak the things which we have* **seen** *and* **heard** (Acts 4:20).

They had *seen* Jesus heal the sick, cast out devils, give sight to the blind, raise the paralytic, bless the poor. They were His witnesses!

They had *heard* Him say, "The things which I do shall you do also. Go. Heal the sick, cast out devils, preach the Gospel. As My Father has sent Me into the world, even so send I you."

They had *seen* His example and *heard* His orders to do likewise. Therefore, they said, *We cannot but speak the things which we have seen and heard.*

Thank God that, as Gospel messengers today, we can have that same testimony and we can minister on that same principle in our generation.

Jesus said we must take this Gospel to all nations as a witness with evidence. Only men and women full of faith and the power of the Holy Ghost can do this!

Nothing else will substitute for this Gospel with evidence. There exists no substitute for the demonstration of the Spirit and of power.

It is the witness with evidence that convinces!

One demonstration is worth a thousand lectures!

One miracle is worth a thousand sermons!

All Jerusalem was thrown into a tremendous spiritual awakening when the crippled beggar was healed.

The city of Ponce, Puerto Rico, became aware of Christ's power when Juan Santos walked. For sixteen years, he had dragged his body on the ground with his hands. This and other miracles convinced the whole city!

The entire city of Guatemala gave heed to what we preached there when the blind, crazy, paralyzed beggar of their streets was healed instantly. He was a witness. His case was evidence!

The entire city of Nakuru, Kenya, acknowledged the power of Jesus Christ when the little boy, Simeon, who was born without eyeballs, received a creative miracle. New eyeballs were formed within a few hours and his sight became normal.

This Gospel of the Kingdom was preached as a witness!

I have spoken of the pioneers of the Early Church because they were successful. Whole cities changed. Whole multitudes believed. Whole countries were affected. *So mightily grew the word of God and prevailed* (Acts 19:20).

When the methods of the Early Church met with such response and produced such miraculous results, let us never substitute other methods which have never prospered.

There is such abundant evidence that the methods of the Early Church, if applied today, will produce the same results as in Bible days. Therefore, let us resolve that since Jesus Christ is the same yesterday, today, and forever, we too can proclaim His Word with simple faith and, by acting on God's promises, can receive the same results in our generation.

Fashions change! Times change! Styles change! Theories change! Doctrines change! Religions change!

But, **this Gospel was designed by the Master to be proclaimed without alteration or adjustment to every creature, to all nations, unto the end of the world.**

We need not conform the Gospel to a modern mentality. We need only to proclaim this Gospel of the Kingdom as a *witness with miracle evidence,* and the same results will follow today as did in the Early Church: Believers were added to the Church *daily,* multitudes of both men and women.

16
Miracles Around the World

I write this as one who knows what it means to proclaim the Gospel in total simplicity in nearly seventy nations during more than three glorious decades.

I know what it means to obey God rather than man. I have done it!

I know what it means for men to discourage and condemn one who dares to be bold in the ministry. They have done it to me!

But I also know that **faith will win** and **bold courage will defeat every enemy.**

I am a witness to the fact that **it pays to obey God** rather than men.

I have felt the pulse beat of suffering humanity around the world and have had the privilege of pointing hundreds of thousands of precious souls to the loving arms of Jesus.

I have proven the truth of this statement: **There is only one way to evangelize the world before Jesus comes. The only way is to proclaim this Gospel with evidence in the power of the Holy Spirit that confirms it with miracles.**

I am convinced that **there exists a yearning in the hearts of every people,** regardless of race or color, **to know and to serve the God of miracles.** . . . (God) *hath made of one blood all nations of men for to dwell on all the face of the earth* (Acts 17:26); and they all have the same hunger for the God Who confirms His Word and fulfills His promises with signs, miracles, and wonders.

I have preached to Hindus, Moslems, Shintoists, Confucianists, animists, fettishists, and to peoples of many tribal religions.

I have preached in the cold North and in the Deep South, in the traditional East and in the industrialized West.

I have preached to the educated and to the illiterate, to the black, red, yellow, brown, and white.

One thing I know: **All** people of **all** races, of **all** countries, of **all** creeds, have **the same hunger for truth.** All are ready to accept the Christ of the Gospels and serve Him **when they see His Word confirmed by signs and miracles.**

While the modernists and pious theologians warn people to "beware false prophets and deceivers," multiplied thousands of souls, the world over, are turning from traditional religions to serve the Living God, upon hearing the Gospel preached with *evidence*.

Certainly, deceivers will come. But that simply underscores the urgent need for the real power of God in demonstration. He who warns against false miracles should at least produce the real miracles! Moses did, Paul did, Elijah did, Peter did!

17
Miracles for Everybody

There is no difference between the Jew and the Greek: for the same Lord over all is rich unto all that call upon him.

For whosoever shall call upon the name of the Lord shall be saved.

Romans 10:12,13

Miracles are for everybody. The Gospel is for everyone, all the world, every creature, every nation, whosoever. *Everything that Christ died for is available to everyone for whom He died. There are no exceptions with God.*

If ten thousand sinners hear the Gospel of salvation, believe it, repent of their sins and accept Jesus

Christ as their personal Savior by faith, everyone of them will be saved.

If ten thousand sick people hear the Gospel of healing, believe it, resist their sickness and accept Jesus Christ as their personal Healer by faith, everyone of them will be healed.

Jesus died for everybody. He paid the price for everybody to be able to come to God and to receive His gift of life. That must be our message to everybody.

18
Miracles for You

Jesus said, *Preach the Gospel to EVERY creature* (Mark 16:15). That includes **you**.

What is the "Gospel?" It is the Good News of what Jesus did for every person in His substitutionary death on the Cross.

He bore *your* sins so you do not have to bear them; so you can be forgiven **now**.

He did that for *every sinner*—including **you**.

He bore *your* diseases so you do not have to bear them; so you can be healed **now**.

He did that for *every sick person*—including **you**.

He bore *your* pains so that you do not have to bear them; so you can be relieved **now**.

He did that for *every sufferer*—including **you**.

Everything Jesus Christ did in His death as our *Substitute*, He did so that we do not have to do it.

That is why miracles are for you.

Jesus died so that **you** can have life.

Jesus was sick so that **you** can have health.

Jesus was made our sin so that **you** can be righteous.

Therefore, every miracle He died to provide is for YOU—NOW.

He took your sins and gives you His righteousness **now** (2 Cor. 5:21).

He bore your diseases and gives you His health **now** (Is. 53:4,5).

He carried away your weaknesses and gives you His strength **now**.

That is why miracles are for YOU—NOW.

He already took your sins. Believe it and be saved **now**.

He already took your diseases. Believe it and be healed **now**.

Everything Christ accomplished at the Cross is part of the "Gospel" —part of the "Good News." *It is for "every creature" right NOW—and that includes YOU.*

This is the Gospel that we must preach with evidence. This is the Gospel Jesus Christ confirms with signs and wonders. This is the Gospel that is *the power of God unto salvation to EVERY ONE that believeth* (Rom. 1:16).

If you are not included, no one can be included. If salvation is not for you, it can be for no one. If healing is not provided for you, it is not for anyone.

But all of God's miracles are for you!

And, *NOW is the accepted time; . . . NOW is the day of salvation* (2 Cor. 6:2) for YOU, if you have not accepted Christ by faith or if you need His miracle blessings.

Now is the time to accept all of the blessings Jesus died to provide.

The Bible says, *AS MANY as received him, to them gave he power to become the sons of God* (John 1:12). **That includes YOU—NOW.**

The Bible says, *AS MANY as touched him were made whole* (Mark 6:56). **That includes YOU—NOW.**

MIRACLES

Photographs

MULTITUDES AND MIRACLES

This Osborn Crusade in Nigeria is typical of the multitudes which have been drawn to hear the Gospel *confirmed by miracles*, in nearly seventy nations during over three decades of their miracle evangelism ministry.

"A great multitude followed him, because *they saw his miracles* which he did on them that were diseased" (John 6:2).

"And the people with one accord gave heed unto those things which Philip spoke, *hearing and seeing the miracles* which he did . . . And there was great joy in that city" (Acts 8:6,8).

CRIPPLED 23 YEARS

Peter Amakanji had never stood on his feet in 23 years. Crippled by polio when he was a baby, his legs were left useless and withered.

All of his life, he had scooted himself about on his buttocks, by using his hands.

He was brought to the Osborn Crusade in Nakuru, Kenya, where he heard the Gospel and believed on Christ. He was instantly healed and within a few days, his legs actually grew to normal size. (Before, he said, they were like wet ropes.)

At the side of T. L. Osborn, and on the crusade platform (photos), Peter had become an evangelist—a living **witness**—walking **evidence** of the Gospel —**proof** that Jesus Christ is alive—**now**.

LEG GROWS FOUR INCHES

Little Yolanda Cordova was born with one leg shorter than the other, the result of a malformation in the fetus. As she grew, her right leg had become four inches shorter than the left one and was paralyzed. A special shoe with a four-inch extension, coupled to a heavy foot-to-hip steel brace, helped her to walk.

Brought to the Osborn Crusade in Bogota, Colombia, by her desperate mother, the child was miraculously healed as Mr. Osborn prayed a mass prayer for the multitude of over 100,000 people.

Shown in the lower photo are many others in the vast Bogota crowd who discarded crutches, braces, and other aids after being instantly healed through their own faith which they received listening to the Gospel.

MINISTRY OF MIRACLES

Scenes like these (opposite page), captured during the Osborn Crusade in Mexico, are reminiscent of Bible days when *they brought unto him many that were possessed with devils: and he cast out the spirits with his word, and healed all that were sick* (Matt. 8:16).

Great multitudes came together to hear, and to be healed by him of their infirmities . . . And it came to pass . . . as he was teaching . . . the power of the Lord was present to heal (Luke 5:15,17).

T. L. Osborn believes that God's power is in His Word. Most of the great miracles he has witnessed worldwide have taken place as the people heard him teach and received faith to be healed out in the multitude—like these cases (see photos). *He sent his word, and healed them* (Ps. 107:20).

Miracles give proof of the Gospel.

MIRACLES —
PROOF OF GOD'S POWER

T. L. Osborn holds the braces and crutches of someone healed in the multitude (top photo), who had passed them over the heads of the people to the evangelist. While waiting for that person to arrive at the platform to testify, he signals another pair of crutches being held aloft—another miracle that God had wrought among the crowd.

The woman who had passed her crutches and braces up to Mr. Osborn finally got through the press of people to show what God had done. Having been crippled by polio as a child, she had been left paralyzed. Now her legs are strong.

Thousands glorified God saying, as the people did in Capernaum, *We never saw it on this fashion* (Mk. 2:12).

THE JUAN SANTOS MIRACLE

Shot through the spine, Mr. Juan Santos was left totally paralyzed from his waist down, with shaking palsy in his upper body. For 16 years he dragged himself along, using his hands and a small box which he would rest on when he stopped.

He was carried to the Osborn Crusade where he heard the Gospel and saw it confirmed by miracles. For the first time, he learned that what Jesus did in Bible days, He will do today.

He believed on the Lord and was instantly and totally healed. The entire city was astounded by this notable miracle.

Mr. Santos became a living witness for Christ by going from town to town and showing how the Lord miraculously healed him. Thousands believed the Gospel because of this **living proof of God's power.**

The Osborn World Ministry

The ministry of T. L. Osborn has made an unprecedented impact on the world in our time. He is regarded by many as one of the greatest soulwinners of this Century.

As young missionaries, T. L. and his wife, Daisy, determined to take the Gospel of Jesus to the unreached multitudes. In the years since, they have pioneered many effective methods and tools which have enabled them and thousands of other Christian workers and National church leaders to accomplish this goal.

Early in their ministry overseas, when first confronted by immense crowds, the Osborns introduced the concept of successfully praying for the sick *en masse*. In one of those early crusades, 125 deaf mutes and 90 totally blind people were miraculously healed by the power of God.

T. L. Osborn is an energetic and prolific writer. His special series of 18 Gospel tracts have been published in 132 languages and distributed at the rate of over a ton a day for many years. He has authored several powerful books, including the living classic, *Healing the Sick*.

The Osborns have ministered in nearly seventy nations and their team effort in missions is unequalled as they preach the Good News to the world: that *Jesus Christ is the same yesterday, to day, and for ever* (Heb. 13:8).

Available from Harrison House
Books by T. L. Osborn

Soulwinning
Healing the Sick
Miracles — Proof of God's Power
How To Be Born Again
The Good Life
How To Receive Miracle Healing
In His Name
Join This Chariot
Purpose of Pentecost
When Jesus Visited Our House

Harrison House • P.O. Box 35035 • Tulsa, OK 74135

* Visit the Osborn International Headquarters
* Discover Mid-America's World Landmark

Request a list of Osborn Mass Crusade and Teaching Cassettes.
Also available, **Faith Digest**, Osborn's Magazine.

Write: T. L. Osborn
Box 10
Tulsa, OK 74102

I would like to receive T. L. Osborn's
exciting publication,
FAITH DIGEST,
free and postpaid to my home.

NAME (PLEASE PRINT)

ADDRESS

CITY   *STATE*   *ZIP*

Whon completed, tear out
this coupon and mail to:

T. L. & Daisy Osborn
Box 10
Tulsa, OK 74102

---

*Please include your
prayer requests and comments
on the reverse side.*